# THE
# BRITISH
# ISLES

# Cultures and Costumes Series:

CULTURES AND COSTUMES: SYMBOLS OF THEIR PERIOD

# THE
# BRITISH
# ISLES

CHARLOTTE GREIG

MASON CREST PUBLISHERS

www.masoncrest.com

Mason Crest Publishers Inc.
370 Reed Road
Broomall, PA 19008
(866) MCP-BOOK (toll free)
www.masoncrest.com

First printing 2002

1 2 3 4 5 6 7 8 9 10

Library of Congress Cataloging-in-Publication Data available

ISBN 1-59084-431-9

Printed and bound in Malaysia

Editorial and design by
Amber Books Ltd.
Bradley's Close
74–77 White Lion Street
London N1 9PF

**Project Editor:** Marie-Claire Muir
**Designer:** Hawes Design
**Picture Research:** Lisa Wren

**Picture Credits:**
**All pictures courtesy of Amber Books Ltd,** except the following:
**Mary Evans Picture Library:** 8, 49.

**ACKNOWLEDGMENT**
For authenticating this book, the Publishers would like to thank
Robert L. Humphrey, Jr., Professor Emeritus of Anthropology,
George Washington University, Washington, D.C.

# Contents

Scotland

Northern
Ireland

Ireland

Wales

England

The British Isles are made up of
two main islands: Britain and
Ireland. Britain itself is divided
into England, Scotland, and Wales.
During the last Ice Age, Britain
was joined to Europe by a wide
land bridge across what is now
the English Channel.

# Introduction

Nearly every species in the animal kingdom adapts to changes in the environment. To cope with cold weather, the cat adapts by growing a longer coat of fur, the bear hibernates, and birds migrate to a different climatic zone. Only humans use costume and culture—what they have learned through many generations—to adapt to the environment.

The first humans developed their culture by using spears to hunt the bear, knives and scrapers to skin it, and needles and sinew to turn the hide into a warm coat to insulate their hairless bodies. As time went on, the clothes humans wore became an indicator of cultural and individual differences. Some were clearly developed to be more comfortable in the environment, others were designed for decorative, economic, political, and religious reasons.

Ritual costumes can tell us about the deities, ancestors, and civil and military ranking in a society, while other clothing styles can identify local or national identity. Social class, gender, age, economic status, climate, profession, and political persuasion are also reflected in clothing. Anthropologists have even tied changes in the hemline length of women's dresses to periods of cultural stress or relative calm.

In 13 beautifully illustrated volumes, the *Cultures and Costumes: Symbols of their Period* series explores the remarkable variety of costumes found around the world and through different eras. Each book shows how different societies have clothed themselves, revealing a wealth of diverse and sometimes mystifying explanations. Costume can be used as a social indicator by scientists, artists, cinematographers, historians, and designers—and also provide students with a better understanding of their own and other cultures.

ROBERT L. HUMPHREY, JR., Professor Emeritus of Anthropology,
George Washington University, Washington, D.C.

ANGLORVM ETSVI MILITES :EQVI TANT: AD BOS    HA

HIC   HAROLD   MARE    NAVIGAVIT   ETVE    LIS

# Early Britain

**As the culture of the British Isles advanced out of the mists of prehistory, costume evolved as knowledge grew and other peoples invaded and settled. Simply sewn Neolithic skins and Bronze Age breeches gave way to ornately fashioned Celtic weapons and more specialized garments of wool, linen, and even—for the richest—cloth of gold.**

The early inhabitants of the British Isles during the Stone Age are thought to have worn little clothing other than animal skins wrapped around the body. Over time, Stone Age people in Britain began to make simple clothes of animal skins. The skins were cleaned with scrapers made of flint and then sewn together with bone needles, using thread made of animal **sinews**. There is evidence that shoes were being made from around 7000 B.C. (the Mesolithic period), and that from around 4000 B.C. (the early Neolithic age) gold jewelry and pottery were made. During the Neolithic era, a major change occurred in Britain as tribes settled and began farming. They made tools of flint and traded these; however, there is no evidence of weaving or spinning before the Bronze Age in about 2000 B.C.

Bronze Age men wore belted leather **breeches** with long strips of leather wrapped around the lower leg in a crisscross fashion. They also wore rough

**The Bayeux Tapestry, completed in about 1092, shows more than 70 scenes of the invasion of Britain by the Normans from France in 1066. The Normans brought sophisticated court fashions to Britain for the first time.**

9

shoes made of animal skin and laced together at the front. They often went bare-chested, but over their shoulders they wore a small cloak of leather or wool. The women wore long or short woolen tunics over a woolen underskirt, with a square blanket as a cloak, fastened at the shoulder by a pin or clasp.

## Ancient Britons

In 55 B.C., the Roman army came to Britain under Julius Caesar. By this time, in common with the rest of Europe, the people of Britain were making and using iron tools. (Hence this period is called the Iron Age.) The Romans called the natives of Britain, and any other tribes outside Roman rule, "northern barbarians." Much of our knowledge about these peoples comes from Caesar's description of them.

By the time of Caesar's arrival in Britain, the natives of the country, influenced by settlers from Europe, were producing dyed woolen cloth. The cloth was patterned with stripes and plaids, and was rough on one side. The colors used were usually dark blue, red, and black. The men wore woven **tunics**,

**This Bronze Age chieftain has a bronze helmet decorated with a white heron's feather. His tunic, cloak, and leggings are made of white wool, indicating his high status.**

# Bronze Age Jewelry

During the Bronze Age (so-called because bronze was used for making tools and weapons), people began to bury their dead in individual graves, often with belongings, such as pottery. Some of the articles in these early graves have survived and have been identified by **archaeologists**, who have traced their history. For example, archaeologists have identified a culture they call the Beaker People by looking at ancient remains of pottery found in early graves. Other items from early Bronze Age cultures have also been found, including bronze, gold, amber, and **jet** armbands and necklaces. In one grave, a chief was found buried in a shoulder cape made entirely of gold. Fragments of woolen cloth and flax (fiber from the flax plant used for weaving linen) have also been found.

trousers, and pants, and the crisscross leather strips were still worn over the trousers. Men also wore fur or woolen caps and sleeveless fur jackets for warmth. The women wore their hair long, either loose or braided. They wore long, belted woolen tunics, shoes, and woolen cloaks fastened with large carved **brooches**.

**A man from the late Paleolithic era wears a tunic made of animal skin and carries a wooden spear and club. At this time, flint was used to make tools and weapons.**

**This warrior's gold helmet features a horsehair plume. His military tunic and cloak are made of red wool. Warriors like these fought the Romans, who called them "barbarians."**

## Celtic Culture

The Celts were members of an early people with ancestors from both India and Europe. From the second millennium B.C., they spread over many parts of northern Europe and the British Isles, displacing or ruling over Neolithic peoples in these areas. They are thought to have originated in Austria and to have become a powerful group by trading along the great rivers of Europe. One of the reasons they became so powerful was that they introduced iron to the European tribes.

The Celts were warlike people with many tribes or bands, who, from about 400 B.C., raided and ransacked many cities and civilizations, including Rome in Italy and Delphi in Greece. They were eventually subdued by the Romans under Julius Caesar. Today, little of their culture survives except their languages, which can be traced back through the native languages of Ireland, Scotland, and Wales. In recent years, there has been a revival of these languages in the British Isles, along with renewed interest in the artistic culture of the Celts.

"La Tène" culture, as European Celtic art is called (named after an archaeological site in Switzerland), originated in the fifth century B.C. It is characterized by round, symmetrical lines and curving S shapes, as well as spiral and knot patterns. These designs come from many sources. For example, the Celtic cross, a cross within a circle, is thought to come from Hindu mythology. There are also symbols from Greek and Etruscan art in Celtic designs.

The Celts settled in Britain from the eighth century B.C. onward, migrating from Austria and other parts of Europe, and establishing a new farming system. They also built many hill forts, suggesting that there was resistance to them from the local population of Britons. A British form of Celtic art was developed, mostly to decorate weapons of war, such as swords, scabbards (the sheath for holding a sword), shields, spears, and helmets. Later, tribes of Gauls arrived from what is now France, escaping from German and Roman colonizers. The Gauls added their influence to the British form of Celtic art.

## Roman Influences

In Britain, Roman soldiers adopted the Britons' crisscrossed leather breeches, calling them *braccatae*. They wore these *braccatae* underneath their tunics.

During Roman rule in Britain, which lasted until A.D. 410, many Britons adopted Roman styles of dress. In addition to their traditional clothes, Britons now wore the practical hooded cloak of the Romans, the *paenula*. The women also began to wear long, white, linen tunics. To keep warm in the British climate, they wore woolen tunics and rectangular woolen cloaks, draping the cloak over the shoulders and head. Women also adopted Roman hairstyles, piling their hair up and fixing it with

**This bronze crown of Celtic origin has a characteristic cross and circle design. In Celtic times, bronze jewelry was often decorated with gold discs and pieces of amber.**

# Celtic Armor

A Greek historian, Diodorus Siculus, who lived at the time of Julius Caesar, wrote a history of the period in which he gave a detailed account of Celtic armor. He describes large bronze shields, decorated with projecting figures that gave extra protection to the soldier, and high bronze helmets, sometimes with horns, which made the wearer look very tall. Soldiers also wore iron breastplates and carried long swords held by iron or bronze chains hanging from the hip. In addition, they carried huge spears with large iron heads on them, some twisted into spiral forms so that, as well as cutting flesh, they would tear it into pieces. Warriors also wore decorative gold- or silver-plated belts.

carved pins made of bone. In the upper classes, both sexes wore crafted leather Roman sandals instead of the roughly made shoes of earlier times.

In Roman Britain, dress became a sign of social status, as it was in Rome and elsewhere in the Roman Empire. Workers wore loose tunics and rough shoes, while those of higher social status wore the Roman **toga**, made of white wool instead of linen. A colored band around the neck and hem showed what class the wearer belonged to; for example, magistrates (civil administrators of the law) wore togas bordered with purple.

During the Roman occupation of Britain, the craft of spinning developed as upright looms and weighted spindles began to be used. Fine cloth was made, and domestic life improved in most parts of the country. However, after the fall of the Roman Empire in A.D. 410, Britain entered a more primitive level of civilization, called the Dark Ages.

## Saxon Dress

In the fifth and sixth centuries A.D., Germanic peoples such as the Jutes (from Jutland—modern-day Denmark—and the Rhineland), the Saxons, and the Angles (from Northern Germany), migrated to Britain and settled in small

**This woman from ancient Britain wears a long white tunic, a woolen underskirt, and simple shoes. Her cloak is worn over her head in a style adopted from the Romans.**

villages and towns. The Anglo-Saxons, as they are now called, fought the Britons for land, but there were also peaceful settlements of farmers and craftsmen, who lived alongside the native peoples. The immigrants brought with them new languages and new social systems. Most Anglo-Saxons were either freemen or slaves; the freemen owned land and slaves. The richest freemen were called thanes and were closely associated with the main ruler, the king. During this period, England became a kingdom, but there was a lot of conflict and unrest as the thanes battled for power, and the British Isles became less civilized and ordered than they had been under the Romans.

In Roman times, clothing had as much to do with fashion as with practicality, at least for the upper classes. By contrast, the Saxons dressed for warmth and for ease of movement. Both men and women wore tunics with tight, wrinkled sleeves that could be pulled down to keep the hands warm. Unlike Roman houses, which had central heating systems, Saxon houses were cold. Instead of the Roman sandal, Saxons wore rough shoes laced at the front like those of the ancient Britons. Saxon men wore their hair long, and their beards were parted in the center. Anglo-Saxons began to convert to Christianity in the seventh century, and women began to cover their heads, wearing close-fitting caps with a padded or rolled edge, covered by a hooded cloak or veil.

Although the Anglo-Saxons were not a highly cultured people, there was a high standard of embroidery for clothes worn by the thanes and kings. The gold embroidery used on their cloaks and tunics became known in Europe as "English work." Meanwhile, noblewomen wore ornate gold, garnet, and amethyst jewelry, often in the shape of a cross.

## Norman Fashions

In 1066, the Normans from France, under William the Conqueror, invaded Britain and took control of the country. The Normans brought with them a new language, new customs, and a more sophisticated style of dress. In general, Norman clothes were more elaborately styled than those of the Saxons, with long, flowing robes and different types of ornament. However, these changes in fashion affected only the nobility and upper classes, who did not do a great deal of manual work. For the common laborer, clothing had to remain much the same as it was in Saxon times.

Upper-class men and women wore *sabbatons*, shoes with long points that were stuffed with wool. As the popularity of this fashion increased, the points became longer, until they reached several inches beyond the toe. The *sabbatons* were usually made of dyed leather and embroidered on the front. However, **serfs**, or common people, continued to wear rough leather shoes or ankle-length boots laced at the front or around the ankle.

**This 10th-century Norman knight wears a protective coat with iron rings sewn into the material. The rings are not interlinked, as with chainmail, but they still provide an effective defence.**

Under William the Conqueror, nobles wore their hair short and were clean-shaven, while serfs had long hair and beards. Norman gentlemen wore a linen tunic called a *justaucorps* under a short-sleeved woolen tunic; over this was a cloak fastened at one shoulder with a ring. They also wore leggings made of soft wool, linen, or leather. Noblewomen wore a long-sleeved linen **chemise**, or *sherte*, under a gown with a long, hanging girdle—a type of fabric belt—at the waist. A mantle, or cloak, was worn over the shoulders, fastened with an ornamental clasp and a piece of cord. Like the Saxon Christian women, Norman women covered their heads with a piece of cloth and a band tied around to secure it. They also braided their long hair.

## The Sumptuary Laws

During the medieval period, which lasted from the middle of the 12th century to the end of the 15th century, fashion reached a high point in England. This was partly because of the Crusades, wars in which Christian powers from Europe tried to capture parts of the Holy Land from the Muslims who lived there. English kings brought back treasures from the East, such as beautiful silks, creating a great demand for this new luxury fabric among the wealthy English nobility. Fashion changed more slowly among the common people, who did not have the means to buy expensive cloth and tailored clothing.

Eventually, churchmen became enraged about the passion for high fashion in England, and in 1363, the sumptuary laws were passed. These laws decreed that only royalty and nobility could wear pearl embroidery and ermine (a luxurious kind of fur), that only knights could wear gold cloth, and that only squires (landowners) could wear silver. In addition, the laws stated that common people were not allowed to wear any jewelry at all, or any fine wool or silk clothing—even if they could afford it. The sumptuary laws showed that, by this time, clothing had become an important sign of social status in England, and that costume was a complex, detailed, and tightly controlled way of showing a person's exact position, income, and occupation.

# Scotland, Ireland, and Wales

**The inhabitants of Scotland, Ireland, and Wales are often known as the Celtic peoples. Their ancient languages are related to each other, and their history goes back to the Celtic tribes of Europe. Their cultures, especially in music, are distinct, and their national costumes give a strong sense of their independent past.**

Over the centuries, there has been a great deal of conflict in the British Isles over the matter of English rule, which Scotland, Wales, and especially Ireland have fought to gain independence. Today, only the large southern part of Ireland is a separate state from the rest of Great Britain, but the Celtic parts of the British Isles have retained a strong identity of their own.

## Scottish Tartan

The early Celtic tribes in Scotland were known for their high-quality woolen cloth, dyed with vegetable dyes, such as madder (for red), woad (for blue), and

**Members of the Scottish aristocracy and royalty are shown (left) in their finery. For court, the "lairds" (lords) wore coats and doublets in Spanish and French styles with their Scottish kilts.**

weld (for yellow). The cloth was woven on looms and patterned with stripes and plaids (called checks by the British). By 1471, a cloth known as tartan, or *breachan* (meaning "checkered" in Gaelic), had developed. Tartans have plaid patterns made by mixing colors and threads together so that, as well as blocks of each separate color (for example, red and blue), there are blocks of mixed colors (for example, purple—a mixture of red and blue). Additionally, there are variations in the size of the blocks, with small blocks running alongside larger ones. The overall effect is a subtle blend of color and pattern. Even when bold colors are used, they are run together so that they make a blended whole.

As the technology and skills of Scottish weavers improved, various districts developed individual styles of pattern and color. In this way, a particular weave came to be identified with a group of clans, or families, living in the same area. Later, special weaves were chosen to represent military regiments, so that a soldier could be recognized by the tartan uniform he was wearing. The dark Black Watch tartan came to be used as the government uniform, and it is now the tartan of the Royal Highland regiment of the British army.

## The Banning of Tartan

In Scotland, there were many clans that wanted the British Isles to be ruled by Scottish kings and queens (the Stuarts). These clans united under Bonnie Prince Charlie, the grandson of King James II, a Catholic king of England who had been exiled. To show their support for the prince, the Jacobites, as his followers were called, wore a white feather called a cockade in their hats.

In 1746, an uprising of the Jacobites was put down and the Highland clans were disarmed. The following year, the English passed a law forbidding the wearing of tartan. In 1782, the act was repealed, but by this time the "setts" and "pattern sticks" used by weavers to make special clan patterns had been lost or destroyed. However, some fragments of the original tartans remained, and there was a great effort to revive them. The Highland military regiments of the 18th century wore tartan as part of their uniform. In the early 19th century, the

**This Highland archer of the MacQuaaries clan wears a kilt or *feileadh beag* (little wrap). His doublet features slashes at the shoulders, in the style fashionable at the time.**

English king, George IV, encouraged the revival of the tartan, especially for military wear.

From the 19th century on, tartan became established in Scotland in a systematic way, with special tartans for each family name—for example, Stuart, Campbell, and Macgregor, to name but a few. In 1963, a registry of tartans was set up and recorded over 1,000 different patterns, or setts. In some cases, clans or families have two types of tartan: a bright one for formal occasions and a more muted one, called a hunting sett, for everyday wear in the Highlands.

## The Kilt

In the 13th century, the Scottish Highlander wore a tunic known as the saffron shirt, quilted with wool and smeared with grease to make it waterproof. It is now thought that this tunic was not dyed with saffron, which was an expensive Eastern dye, but with a kind of moss or lichen that is common in Scotland. By the end of the century, this style went out of favor and was replaced by the plaid, which means "blanket" in Gaelic. This was a rectangular length of cloth worn over the shoulder and belted at the waist so that the lower half reached the knees. In cold weather, this large garment would also be used to cover the head and the upper half of the body. Later on, the plaid was replaced by the smaller kilt, a skirtlike length of tartan cloth, long enough to reach to the knees, belted around the waist, and sewn in pleats at the back. The kilt was called the *feileadh beag*, or "little wrap," to distinguish it from the *feileadh mor*, the "big wrap," or belted plaid.

Until recently, scholars thought that an English industrialist, Thomas Rawlinson, who owned an ironworks in Scotland in the 18th century, had invented the kilt. It was thought that Rawlinson had made his workers cut down their belted plaids to the more practical kilt to avoid getting the big plaids caught in the machinery. However, illustrations have now been found that show Highlanders wearing kilts earlier than this date. This new

**The saffron shirt was worn by men of high birth in 13th-century Scotland. The leafy twig on this soldier's helmet shows his allegiance to the Ferguson clan.**

# Scottish Legend and Myth

Since the Victorian period (1837–1901), Scottish history has excited the popular imagination. Bonny Prince Charlie, for example, has become a legendary figure. After the failure of the Jacobite rebellion of 1745, Bonny Prince Charlie escaped to France. He tried to revive interest in his claim, but ended up a drunken, bitter man with few followers. However, he has since become a hero of Scottish ballads and legends, and his story is seen as one of romance and adventure.

In the same way, the history of Scottish costume has been romanticized. Today, there is a large industry selling kilts and other items of Scottish dress. In particular, many tartans are made, each one representing a clan or sept. A clan is a family name, such as Macgregor, and a sept is a name related to the main clan, such as Gregory. Buyers are encouraged to trace their family name's relation to the main clan, and then to match a tartan to their name. They will then buy kilts, ties, plaid rugs, shawls, and many other items displaying their tartan.

However, there is, in fact, little historical evidence for the idea that each and every clan in Scotland had its own tartan. There are few portraits of chiefs and lairds (lords) wearing their tartans before the 19th century; apart from those painted in military dress of tartan kilts, most of them wear the clothes of the British nobility of the time. Also, clans were not generally recognized by their tartans, as legend would have it; clan members usually wore a plant in their bonnet to show which family they came from. This was especially helpful in battle, because the upright plant was easily visible.

Perhaps we should see the tracing, choosing, and wearing of "family" tartans today as, in most cases, an enjoyable pastime rather than as serious historical research.

**This soldier from the Maclaurin clan is wearing the *feileadh mor* (big wrap), or belted plaid. He also wears a conical helmet and a silk doublet underneath his chain mail.**

research has been a great relief to the Scots, who did not like to think that an Englishman had invented their national dress.

Today, many Scotsmen have adopted the kilt as national dress for formal occasions and for special events, such as soccer matches. The Scottish national dress is usually a kilt in a dark green tartan, with a sporran at the front hanging from a belt. The sporran is a fur pouch or bag with tassels on it. The kilt is worn with a stylish, fitted black jacket with silver buttons at the front, back, and cuffs; this jacket is known as the Prince Charlie, after the last Scottish prince to lay claim to the English throne. Under the jacket a tie is sometimes worn, but more often, a lace jabot (neck cloth); lace cuffs are also sewn or snapped into the jacket. On the legs, long woolen socks with garters at the knee are worn; the long ends, or flashes, of the garters hang down at the side of the knee. A small, sheathed dagger called a *skean-dhu* is tucked into the right-hand garter. There are also several different kinds of light dress shoes, or gillies, with silver-gilt buckles or long laces that tie around the front of the foot and the ankle. A broad, flat hat, or bonnet, with a pom-pom is also sometimes worn.

## Women's Dress: The *Arisaid*

Like the men, in early times, women also wore the "big wrap," or plaid. For women, this large, blanket-like garment was worn long, like a cloak, to the

**This Scotswoman is from the Urquhart clan. She wears the *arisaid*, a long women's plaid belted at the waist and designed to cover the wearer from head to toe.**

heels. It was belted at the waist in such a way that folds hung over the belt. The *arisaid*, as the female plaid was called, was fastened at the breast by a brooch. Strangely enough, given the fact that the *arisaid* covered most of the female body, this garment was sometimes associated with loose, immoral behavior. In the early 17th century, it was reported that women used the *arisaid* to cover their heads in "kirk" (the Scottish word for church), so that they could sleep during the sermon—to the fury of the priests, who tried to ban the wearing of the *arisaid* in church.

## The Irish *Leine*

There are many similarities between Irish and Scottish clothing. In early times, generations of Irish people emigrated to Scotland, bringing their costume and culture with them. Most of them settled in the Scottish Highlands, displacing the native population, the Picts.

From the Book of Kells, an illuminated manuscript of the Gospels that dates from the eighth century A.D., we learn that Irish men and women of importance wore a long fitted tunic called a *leine* and a long, outer cloak called a *brat*. The *brat* also served as a blanket to cover the wearer at night. It is reported that at this time everyone in Ireland, both rich and poor, went barefoot. The peasant folk wore rough clothes, consisting of a shaggy woolen

**An Irish man (left) and woman (right) both wear a long woolen cloak called a "brat" with a woolen *leine,* or tunic, underneath.**

or fur cloak and, for the men, a rough, sleeveless jacket or shirt with leggings (called *trews*). The women wore a long woolen *leine.*

By the 13th century, Irish men and women were wearing *leines* with long, trailing sleeves, a style that persisted for many years. Among the Irish upper class, English fashions of the Tudor kings became popular; for example, the wearing of a white **ruff** around the neck. Later, in the 17th century, Stuart fashions of the Scottish kings, such as tall hats, influenced upper-class Irish dress.

Today, attempts have been made to create an Irish national costume. With the revival of traditional Irish dancing, bright, flamboyant dance clothes are often worn as national dress. Alternatively, kilts are worn as in Scotland—although some believe that the Irish kilt is a modern invention.

## Welsh National Dress

In recent years, there has been a rise in nationalism in Wales, and great efforts have been made to revive the language and culture of this part of the British Isles. Welsh national dress is worn on special occasions, such as Saint David's Day (David, a sixth-century Welsh monk, is the patron saint of Wales) and for the *Eisteddfodd,* a celebration of Welsh song, dance, and poetry that is held every year all over Wales. Women wear a tall hat made of black felt with a small brim around it. Under this is a lace cap with a ruffle around the face. A long gown is also worn, usually with a fitted bodice and full skirt, and a shawl draped over the shoulders. Historically, this style varied from place to place in Wales; in some areas, such as the Gower, shorter black hats, somewhat like top hats, were worn. The fabric of the gown also varied; sometimes it would be black; sometimes it was in black and white plaid. Shawls were commonly made out of red flannel, and a starched white apron was sometimes worn over the gown.

There is no particular national dress for Welsh men. However, a Welsh national tartan has been created in modern times, and tartan trousers or kilts are now worn on special occasions.

**The washerwoman (center) wears a black felt hat, the traditional dress of Welsh women. In many parts of Wales, the hat is taller and is worn with a lace cap.**

# The Common Folk

**In Britain, as in most of the countries of the world, costume has been a way of showing a person's social position and degree of wealth; this has been true throughout history and remains true even today. In the past, however, these differences tended to be more pronounced and were even, in some cases, regulated by law.**

Before the 18th century, it was usually possible to tell what kind of class people belonged to by looking at their clothes. Obviously, wealthy nobles would wear more gold jewelry and fine cloth than common peasants. But there were also strong dress codes among the working classes that showed the type of job they did. For example, a butcher would dress in a certain way, and a carpenter in another. From butcher to carpenter, farmhand to nurse, there were styles of dress that were always worn. These styles changed over the centuries, of course, but in general, the changes were slow. Fashion was associated with the upper classes rather than with the poorer folk, who could not afford to buy or make new clothes regularly.

In addition, the ruling class feared that allowing the lower orders to dress well could cause social unrest. Working people were prevented from wearing fine clothes not just by lack of money and the fear of social disapproval, but also by sumptuary laws, which established exactly what they could and could not wear.

**In medieval times, men wore tunics and hose, with a hooded cape over their shoulders. A hat of straw or felt was often worn on top of the hood.**

In this way, rules about costume were used for many years in Britain as a form of social control to prevent people from moving from one social class to another.

## Peasant Clothing

Under Roman rule, from 54 B.C. to A.D. 410, workmen in the British Isles wore rough, loose tunics. They wore an improved version of the simple shoes, laced at the front, that the ancient Britons had developed. After the fall of the Roman Empire, Britain reverted to less-sophisticated ways until a more civilized pattern of life emerged with the Saxon settlers, starting about A.D. 460.

The Saxon peasant man wore a tunic of rough, woolen cloth, trousers with long garters crisscrossing up the legs, and black leather shoes. Colored leather or embroidery was reserved for the nobles. Saxon women wore a long kirtle (a skirt or dress) with a hooded cloak.

Under Norman rule, from 1066 to 1154, peasant dress changed little. We know some details of soldiers' dress in that period from the Bayeux Tapestry—a great English embroidery work, 19 inches wide by 230 feet long (48 cm by 70 m)—which shows the story of the Norman invasion of England. Norman soldiers wore a hauberk, a hooded tunic with a slit, knee-length lower section to make movement easier. The tunic was made of leather or tough linen and reinforced with leather strips and metal studs. Over the hood, they wore a helmet with a nosepiece. Later, hauberks were made of chain mail.

## Medieval Dress

During the medieval period from 1154 to 1485, the government and the church tightly controlled styles of dressing in an attempt to keep the class system in place. In 1363, it was decreed that commoners could only wear coarse-quality wool and that they could not wear silk or jewels; also, they could not wear long, pointed shoes, which were the fashion of the day. These sumptuary laws remained in force for many years, and were constantly revised and updated as fashions changed.

**In the countryside, laborers wore short tunics that were easy to work in. This picture shows a plowman (left) a man sowing corn (center), and a reaper (right).**

One of the main items of dress in the early medieval period was a long-sleeved tunic called a cotte. Nobles, doctors, and lawyers were allowed to wear the cotte at ankle-length; merchants and traders could wear the garment at mid-calf length; while peasants could only wear it to knee length. Peasants went bareheaded or wore a *chaperon*, a hood that covered the neck and shoulders. Sometimes, the *chaperon* would have a simple scalloped edge at the bottom, but peasants were not allowed to wear the fancy-edged *chaperons* of the upper classes. Peasants also wore wooden clogs over their leather shoes or boots for dirty, muddy work in the farms and fields.

**In medieval times, women as well as men worked as farm laborers. This woman wears a wimple under her hat, and has hitched up her outer skirt for work.**

The peasant woman wore a long-sleeved cotte, often with a striped skirt. On top of this, she wore another dress, a surcote, with short sleeves. The surcote was often hitched up and tied to her belt to allow her to move more freely. Like men, peasant women performed a variety of farm chores. In the towns, servant women wore the cotte with a kirtle, or skirt, underneath. In both town and country, women wore a head covering called a wimple, a piece of cloth draped over the head to frame the face.

Later during the medieval period, the women's cotte and surcote were replaced by the gown, which was usually worn with a kirtle underneath. The kirtle now became a kind of slip or petticoat. Over the front of the gown, which usually had a full skirt, a barme-cloth, or apron, was often worn to try to keep the gown clean while doing domestic work.

## The Yeomen of England

By the end of the medieval period, social life in Britain was changing. Under the medieval **feudal** system, there had been nobles or lords who owned land and serfs, or peasants, who lived and worked on the land. The lord actually owned the serfs; if he sold his land, the serfs were sold with it. In this way, serfs were tied to the land and to their lord, and were effectively slaves.

However, by the end of the 15th century, a new class of independent farmers was emerging. These farmers were called yeomen; they paid rent to the lord, but were not tied to the land like the serfs. In addition, there was a new class of merchants in the towns and cities. These were traders who bought and sold goods that came into Europe through voyages of discovery around the world. A system of commerce and banking was also being evolved.

All these developments meant that society was no longer simply divided between rich and poor, noble and peasant, master and slave. Instead, during the Tudor period from 1485 to 1603, a small middle class of farmers, traders, and bankers came into being. The church and the government, fearful of losing control over the working population, did their best to stop people from moving up from the lower to the new middle classes. One of the ways they did this was through new sumptuary laws, which set out rules of dress for common people.

**The gravedigger on the left is wearing a white undershirt and has rolled up his sleeves for work. He is wearing leg coverings over his bare legs, while his workmate is wearing breeches.**

For men, **doublets** (jackets) and breeches (trousers) had to be in a plain color, not **slashed** with other colors, which was the fashion. Shirts had to be made of plain, unbleached linen with narrow, plain collars, and hose (stockings) had to be made of white wool. Women were not allowed to wear full-length gowns, but could only wear them to mid-calf length. Their caps had to be of plain, white wool, and their shoes had to be low-heeled.

## Roundheads and Cavaliers

During the 17th century, war broke out between the supporters of the king, who wanted absolute power, and the Parliamentarians, who believed that the king should consult Parliament, a group of wealthy landowners. The supporters of the king were called Cavaliers and dressed in fine, showy clothes. The Parliamentarians, who dressed plainly, were known as Roundheads, because of their close-cropped hair. The Roundheads were Puritans who disapproved of the showy, expensive clothes worn in church and at the court; they challenged the authority of both the king and the established church. The Roundheads wanted to establish the English Protestant Church and the English Parliament

# Doublet and Hose

During the Tudor period, the doublet—a short, belted jacket for men—came into fashion. A shirt with a narrow band was worn under the doublet. Peasants and farmers wore simple styles of doublet, along with loose, often badly fitting, hose made of cloth. Shoes were no longer pointed, but rounded at the toes; later in the period, the toes were squared off at the end. For the countrywoman, a gown laced at the back was popular. Under the gown, she wore a chemise, a type of woman's shirt; on her head, she wore a cap called a coif. In the 16th century, both peasant men and women wore tall hats made of coarse felt.

Artist William Hogarth often satirized English manners. The top scene is from *Marriage à la Mode*, published in 1745. The bride is attended by her wig stylist, while the groom, with rollers in his hair, looks on as he sips tea.

# Roundhead Soldiers

At the time of the civil war in England, many of the common men became soldiers. Troopers wore helmets with a back piece shaped in sections, like a lobster tail. Halberdiers, another rank of soldier, wore steel breastplates with a helmet called a comb morion. They carried a long, ax-like weapon. The men also wore plain jerkins (sleeveless and collarless jackets) made of wool or leather over linen shirts with a plain white collar. Their woolen knee breeches were full and baggy. Their shoes featured heavy buckles made of steel (richer people wore silver buckles on their shoes).

as independent bodies, not subject to the rule of the king. After England's Civil War, they established the Commonwealth, a republic without a king, but the king was eventually restored in 1660 when Charles II came to the throne.

With the restoration of the king, servants—both men and women—returned to wearing their hair long, while the upper classes took to wearing wigs. After the restrained dress of the Puritan regime, the upper and middle classes took delight in wearing elaborate, fashionable, and sometimes ridiculous clothes. Servants and country people wore simpler clothing, but added some decorative elements.

## The Industrial Revolution

The 18th century was a time of tremendous change in Britain, as trade and commerce expanded. An

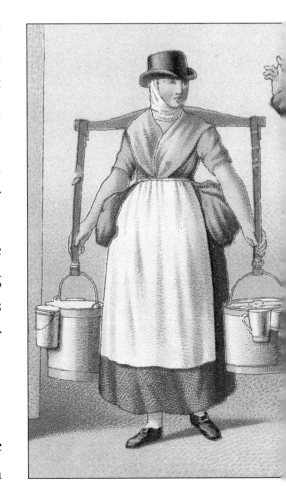

increasingly wealthy middle class began to demand new luxuries, such as tea, coffee, and sugar, which were imported from Britain's colonies around the world. At the same time, technology developed at great speed. Coal mines and factories sprang up all over the country, and the rural population began to move into the towns and cities. The Industrial Revolution, as this change was called, had a great effect on all classes of society, both in the cities and in the countryside.

Most middle-class families of the 18th century had servants. Female servants wore large white caps with a frilly edge called mobcaps; the ladies of the house wore smaller versions of these when indoors. There were

**In the 18th century, street sellers wore distinctive costumes to show their trade, which can be seen in this illustration. From left: a milkmaid, a fireman, a match seller, a newspaper vendor, and a night watchman.**

different types of mobcap, some with an edge that fell to the shoulders, others with a short frill all around and a bow at the front. Over the gown was worn a pinner, or apron. Later in the century, servant women wore a small shawl, called a *fichu*, over the tops of their gowns, crossed over the chest and tied at the waist.

Working men, meanwhile, adopted long vests and jackets, worn with knee breeches and woolen stockings. They wore black tricorne (three-cornered) hats, so-called because the brims were turned back and sewn in three places. Buckled shoes were also worn at this time.

## The Victorians

Under the reign of Queen Victoria, from 1837 to 1901, Britain's empire expanded enormously, bringing in materials from many continents. Britain itself became the largest center of manufacturing and industry in the world, with a huge working class laboring in mines, mills, and factories. These

**A shrimp seller carrying her net (left) and a fish seller at Billingsgate Market in London (right). Both wear the long apron and *fichu,* or shawl, of the female working class.**

**This farmer wears an unbleached linen smock with a slit in the side to make movement easy. This style of dress continued among rural people well into the 19th century.**

workers, who included young children, were poorly housed and clothed. Many of them worked in dangerous, unhealthy conditions.

Fashions for the wealthy classes changed constantly at this time, but working people wore simple clothes. Men wore knee breeches, work shirts, and coarse woolen stockings. Indoors, women wore caps; outdoors, they wore soft hats or bonnets that tied under the chin. Domestic servants usually wore full-skirted gowns and mobcaps in a style that had changed little since the previous century.

In the rural areas, farmers wore linen smocks, large shirts that reached to the knee and were gathered across the chest with embroidery. They also wore gaiters, cloth or leather coverings for the legs that buttoned down one side and were strapped under the foot. Around the neck, farmers often knotted a kerchief or short scarf. Later in the century, farmers began to wear loose vests and trousers that tied at the knees.

By the middle of the century, men began to wear dark clothes in brown, gray, black, or dark blue. Working-class Victorian women also wore dark-colored gowns. This was because smoke from factories made most cities very grimy, and the clothes camouflaged the dirt.

# The Nobility

**From earliest times, chieftains, nobles, and lords dressed more luxuriously than the common people of Britain. But it was with the establishment of the Norman kings in Britain that high fashion for the nobility really took hold.**

Archaeologists have found evidence of gold clothing and jewelry from the Bronze Age, and we know that in the Saxon period, gold embroidery was used to decorate the clothing of thanes (lords). When the Normans from France invaded Britain in 1066, they brought with them sophisticated French fashions, such as sweeping mantles (cloaks) made of soft wool and fastened with ornamental clasps and rings. For women, there were long, trailing girdles (cord belts), laced bodices, and fine head-coverings to wear over their braided hair.

## Ermine and Pearls

During the medieval period, silks and other exotic fabrics were brought to Britain from the East. At the king's court, the new fabrics prompted a craze for fashion and luxurious clothing among the rich and nobly born. Fashions in England came from the king's court and were imitated around the country by lesser nobles and merchants. For example, long trailing sleeves became a court fashion; outside the court, more modest citizens would wear shorter, pointed

**Henry VIII, who reigned from 1509 to 1546, with one of his wives, Anne of Cleves. He wears a robe trimmed with ermine, a style only royalty were allowed to adopt.**

sleeves. Another court fashion was for women to wear a net over their hair; at court, this net would be made of gold or silver; elsewhere, it would be made of less expensive thread.

Court fashion became very elaborate during this period. The more impractical and excessive the garments were, the more they indicated wealth and status. Cloth was made of gold, silver, and velvet; cloaks were trimmed with ermine (the white winter fur of a type of weasel with a black-tipped tail) and miniver (plain white fur). Robes for both sexes were embroidered with pearls and other jewels, while jeweled gloves were worn for hunting and hawking. By about 1325, garments were made of two colors in a style called mi-parti. Noblemen began to wear hose in two colors with a short, belted tunic. Because the tunic was so short, men took to wearing a **codpiece** over the front of their hose to cover their private parts for modesty. Many different types of hat were worn, such as high caps made of white felt, called sugarloaf, or Burgundian caps.

Head coverings were edged with fancy designs in the shape of shells (scalloped), leaves (foliated), or castle turrets (castellated). Hems and sleeves of garments were also decorated in this way. Pointed shoes called crakowes reached such ridiculous lengths that they had to be held up by a string tied to the knee. Women also wore impractical tall steeple hats with a long point at the back, over which was draped a length of fine cloth.

**The short tunics of the 14th century left the legs bare. These were covered with leggings, often in two different colors. Shoes with long points called crakcowes were also worn.**

## The Tudors

Despite the fact that the church constantly complained about the craze for fashion in England, the nobility went on dressing in more fanciful styles during the reign of the Tudor kings and queens, which began in 1485. In 1587, a writer named William Harrison commented on "the fantastical folly of our nation" in following the ever-changing styles at court.

During this period, a short, waisted jacket called a doublet came into fashion for men. It often had padded shoulders, a style also used for women's gowns. These padded sections were slashed with a contrasting color. Around the neck and wrists, both men and women wore ruffs: frilled, stiff collars of white silk and lace. These ruffs reached huge proportions at the court of Queen Elizabeth I, along with a number of other bizarre fashions. For men, there was a padded and peaked doublet called a peasecod, and a type of round hose from the waist to the upper legs called a melon. Both these garments were slashed with different-colored fabrics and often heavily embroidered.

Women wore stiff **corsets** made of wood and canvas under their tight bodices; their enormous skirts were held out with farthingales, an underskirt framework of wooden hoops. Around their necks, both men and women wore enormous "millstone" ruffs and high-standing lace collars called whisks. On their feet, they wore shoes called chopines with high, cork platform soles to protect the wearers from muddy roads and to make them look taller.

The construction of these clothes made them difficult to wash, and little attempt was made to do so. Although the Elizabethan **courtiers** dressed in great finery, their clothes, hair, and bodies were actually filthy, and it is likely that they smelled quite unpleasant.

## The Cavaliers

During the 17th century, the Stuart kings came under attack from Oliver Cromwell and the Jacobites, who deposed King James II and set up a republic, called the Commonwealth, in 1649. However, the monarchy was restored in

1660. The conflict between the monarchists, called Cavaliers, and the republicans, called Roundheads, was a conflict of belief and principle, as well as a political power struggle. The Cavaliers believed in the divine right of kings to rule as they pleased. As members of the aristocracy related or connected to the king, they wanted to keep their privileges of wealth and leisure. They enjoyed hunting and dressed flamboyantly, wearing satin clothes, feathered caps, lace ruffles, and rich jewels. They wore their hair long and curled, and often sported pointed beards and mustaches. In contrast, the Roundheads, so-called because of their close-cropped hair, dressed soberly in black and white. They were not aristocrats, but wealthy landowners who wanted more control over the running of the country.

## Courtiers' Costume

King James I, like Elizabeth I, had a great deal of personal influence over styles for the nobility at court. However, there was such hostility toward him during his reign that he lived in constant fear of his life, worried about being shot or stabbed. For this reason, he favored "bombasted" doublets and breeches—garments that were heavily padded with wool, horsehair, or even sawdust. In this way, he thought he might survive being attacked. Because of his position as king, the courtiers around him also adopted this unwieldy style of dress.

Women at court continued to wear enormous farthingales under their skirts, either in a drum or a cartwheel shape. These skirts took up so much room at court functions that the king eventually banned them, and ladies had to wear softer, unstiffened, but still very full, gowns.

By the reign of the next king, Charles I, the high, stiff ruff of the Elizabethans had been transformed into a wide, flat lace collar around the neck called a falling ruff. Noblemen and -women alike wore this style. Men wore wide-brimmed hats and decorated their shoes with **rosettes**; red heels on the shoes were a sign of high rank. Bucket boots, with high, floppy tops in soft leather, also became fashionable.

Noble children wore the same type of clothes as adults, but in miniature versions; these could be uncomfortable and stiff, especially for young children. It was not until the late 18th century that special fashions were created for the children of the nobility.

**Queen Elizabeth I of England reigned from 1558 to 1603. In this illustration, she wears a circular ruff and a fan-shaped collar. Her hair and clothes are decorated with jewels, especially pearls.**

In the 17th century, the nobility adopted very flamboyant styles of dress, wearing feathered hats, satin capes, silk ribbons, and bucket boots. Both sexes wore their hair long and curled.

## Nell Gwynn

After Cromwell's reign, King Charles II was restored to the throne in 1660. After years of Puritan restraint, court fashions became more extreme than ever. Men decorated their clothes with silk ribbons, bows, and lace. They began to shave their heads and wear wigs made of horse and goat hair. At court, Nell Gwynn, an actress with a colorful past, became the king's mistress. Her flirtatious style of dress was much copied. She wore brightly colored, low-cut gowns showing her underwear (a chemise, or ladies' shirt), and her hair was long and curly.

## Powdered Wigs

Wigs were one of the main items of fashion during the 18th century. Both men and women became obsessed with their wigs, setting aside special rooms for the messy job of powdering them with flour. The nobility used face cones to cover

# Beau Brummel on the Scent

At the beginning of the 19th century, the Prince Regent took over the reign of the country from his father, King George III, who appeared to have lost his mind. Among those in his court circle was Beau Brummel, a famous dandy whose style of clothing set the fashion for men of the day. One of his innovations was to suggest that Englishmen should launder their clothes and wash themselves, instead of trying to cover up smells with strong perfumes, as they had done up to that time.

their faces while their servants powdered the wigs. Less-wealthy people powdered their natural hair, stepping outside to do so.

For men, short wigs with a pigtail at the back, tied with a black bow, were worn when on battle campaigns; at home, they wore long curly wigs cascading over their shoulders. Later, the smoother pigtail wigs were worn all the time, often with a bow in the shape of a bag at the back, to keep the powder off the collar. As the century progressed, a variety of wig fashions—such as the "bob," the "cauliflower," and the "hedgehog"—came and went. Dandies, men who dressed elaborately in the height of fashion, also pioneered their own fantastic designs in wigs. Women's wigs and hairstyles also became enormously high, with complicated curls and ringlets. Once again, the aim was to show wealth and position, for these styles were well beyond the means of the lower classes.

In 1796, a new tax on wig powder put a sudden stop to the craze for styling and powdering wigs. A new mood of seriousness took over at court as the French Revolution of 1790 overthrew the decadent, greedy monarch of France. There was now less enthusiasm for shows of wealth and excess among the English aristocracy—not surprisingly, given the fact that so many French nobles had been beheaded in front of baying crowds in Paris. At the same time, the Industrial Revolution was transforming Britain, and the powerful aristocracy was being replaced by a new class of wealthy businessmen who did not care to dress in bright colors, fancy ribbons, and bows to carry out their grim work of overseeing the factories and mines.

## Victorian Fashions

Under Queen Victoria, whose long reign lasted from 1837 to 1901, Britain expanded its empire and a new class of businessmen became powerful. A new monarch who valued sober hard work and modesty in dress replaced the flamboyant, excessive behavior of the Prince Regent and his court.

During this time, men wore dark, durable suits with a long jacket called a frock coat. Trousers, either striped or plaid, were strapped under the shoes. Shirts had high, stiff collars and were worn with **cravats**. Black top hats completed the outfit. Away from the city, wealthy gentlemen wore Inverness capes—plain coats with a cape at the shoulder—and plaid hats with earflaps tied at the top of the head called deerstalkers, made famous by the fictional Victorian sleuth Sherlock Holmes.

For women, fashions were more fanciful. Although sexual morality was strict at this time, women's clothing was actually very flirtatious. Women were required to cover their legs at all times, but they could wear tight, low-cut evening dresses, showing off their shoulders, arms, and bosom. Corsets were tight, emphasizing small waists, which were considered beautiful.

Another feature of Victorian dress that emphasized the female figure was the crinoline. This was a series of bamboo, bone, or metal hoops worn around the waist to push the skirt in a wide circular shape. Sleeves with wide shoulders and narrow cuffs also emphasized the hourglass shape of the woman's body. Toward the end of the 19th century, attention shifted from the front to the back of the body, with the bustle. The bustle was a big drape of fabric with a bow that sat on the woman's behind, which was padded out with horsehair or metal springs. As in years gone by, the more elaborate, impractical, and uncomfortable a costume was, the more it seemed to appeal to the leisured upper classes of society.

# The Empire Line

For women, a new style of soft, feminine dress was adopted. The tight waists and stiff skirts of the past were dropped in favor of loose, high-waisted gowns in the "empire" style, with a ribbon or band under the bust. Soft, flat pumps were worn with the empire gown instead of the heavy, high-heeled buckled shoes of previous years. For outdoors, bonnets made of felt or straw with ribbons that tied under the chin were worn; indoors, the mobcap was still in use. Over the dress, a long coat, or pelisse, was worn, with a decorative shoulder cape known as a pelerine, sometimes trimmed with fur.

**At the beginning of the 19th century, women's fashion imitated the classical styles of the Greeks and the Romans, with long, flowing white dresses and curled hair bound up with ribbons.**

The empire-line dress came into fashion quickly. Just as swiftly, it went out of fashion, and by 1815, skirts were becoming fuller again. However, the flat pumps that had been worn with the empire-line dresses stayed in fashion and were popular during the Victorian era, especially for dancing.

# The Middle Classes

**Before the Industrial Revolution of the 18th century, there was no sizeable middle class in England. However, it quickly grew in importance thanks to the great increase in trade, production, and demand for consumer goods, including fine fabric for clothes.**

A large middle class of businessmen and professionals, such as politicians, lawyers, and doctors, only came into being when great amounts of raw materials and luxury goods began to be imported from the colonies for consumption and manufacture in Britain. This created a new class of wealthy, leisured people, who eventually came to play a more important role in the running of the country than the nobility.

The middle class arose from the merchants and traders who, from earliest times, had brought goods from different parts of the world into the country for sale. Although trading activities had gone on throughout the Roman, Saxon, and Norman eras in Britain, they reached a peak during the medieval period.

**This scene from an 18th-century English middle-class home shows the women wearing mobcaps, while the men sport powdered wigs. Middle-class women only wore their mobcaps indoors.**

**The wimple, made of plain white folded cloth, gave way to more elaborate styles of headdress during the medieval period, including the taller hennin and veil.**

At this time, silk and other luxury fabrics were imported for the first time into the country.

The importing of new materials from abroad created a huge demand for luxurious, fashionable clothes among the nobility. The desire for fine clothes among the aristocracy persisted for centuries, reaching its height at the court of Elizabeth I. However, throughout this period, the class of merchants and traders remained relatively small, serving the much-richer class of aristocrats. During the 17th century, the landed gentry (less-wealthy nobles) gained political power in Britain, but it was not until the 18th century that a middle class began to match the nobility in wealth.

## Medieval Merchants

Merchants in the medieval era in Britain were often finely dressed, especially those who dealt in luxury fabrics and jewelry from abroad. They were usually wealthy people who could afford the best for themselves and their families. Some of the merchants were Jews, who were required by law to wear a yellow cap. Otherwise, they wore clothes similar to those of the nobility, although not so luxurious—for example, garments such as the cote-hardie, a fitted tunic with buttons all the way down the front, and the houppelande, a long, loose tunic with a high collar and padded pleats over the chest that also fastened down the front.

The cote-hardie was often made in the mi-parti style, in which one half of the garment was made in a contrasting color to the other half. Mi-parti hose, in which one leg was a different color from the other, was also fashionable for some years. The houppelande, which might be made of a rich, embroidered fabric, was sometimes left loose and sometimes belted. An aumoniere, or purse for carrying money, was attached to the belt.

On his head, the merchant wore the chaperon, a head covering that also draped over the shoulders, sometimes with a liripipe (a long, pointed hood attached at the back) or a bycocket, a low-crowned hat with a peak at the front. Merchants also adopted the bifid beard, in which the beard was forked into two points.

**The merchant on the right is wearing a chaperon, a head covering. This is also draped over his shoulder. The merchant on the left is wearing a houppelane, a type of loose tunic with a high collar.**

## Tudor Merchants

Under the reign of the Tudor kings, merchants became richer and more important, but they had to be careful not to dress as extravagantly as the nobility, which would have made them unpopular with their masters. The sumptuary laws, which established rules preventing common people from wearing fine clothes, were still in force. However, merchants now began to form a class of people above the common folk but below the aristocracy. Their clothes reflected their status in society. They wore well-cut clothes made of better fabrics than the common man, but without the decorative elements that distinguished the nobles. For example, the sumptuary laws forbade them to slash the sleeves of their clothes with contrasting colors, as was fashionable among the nobility of the time.

The 13th-century merchant wore a loose, ankle-length coat with hanging sleeves, often trimmed with brown fur (ermine and miniver fur were not allowed for commoners). Under this he wore a doublet, a fitted jacket belted at the waist and pleated at the bottom. Under the doublet was a stomacher, a kind of vest, that was attached to his hose. Next to his skin he wore a plain shirt, pleated to a band at the neck; this was plain, unlike the shirts of the nobility, which were embroidered with colored thread. On his head, the merchant wore a square black cap, similar to those worn by the king and his courtiers.

## The Puritans

During the 17th century, the power of the Church of England and the aristocracy came under attack from Oliver Cromwell. Cromwell came from a class of landed gentry, or lesser land-owning nobles, who were critical of the way the monarchy ruled the country, levying heavy taxes to support their extravagant way of life. They wanted to create a more democratic system in which Parliament could run the country's affairs. As Puritans, they also had strong religious beliefs and wanted to further "purify" the Church of England from certain elements that remained from what they saw as greedy, decadent Catholicism, such as ornaments, vestments, and organs. Cromwell was a devout follower of John Calvin, an early Protestant reformer.

After the English Civil War, Cromwell managed to topple the monarchy and establish the Commonwealth in its

## Ruffs and Whisks

Merchants and other citizens wore small ruffs around the neck, but not as large or elaborate as those worn at court. These ruffs could be laundered and starched, and were poked back into shape afterward with a special poking stick.

Merchants' wives also wore simpler versions of the clothes the nobility wore at court. At the beginning of the century, a chemise was worn under a square-necked gown with a shawl around the shoulders that passed under the arms and tied at the waist. Later, a ruff was worn at the neck, and the gown featured padded shoulders. By the end of the century, the gown had a stand-up collar, a simpler version of the whisks worn at court. On her head, the wife wore a cap, or coif; when she went out, she wore different types of headdresses over it, such as a veil with a stiff, peaked **frontlet** framing the face, or a hat made of thrummed (long-haired) felt.

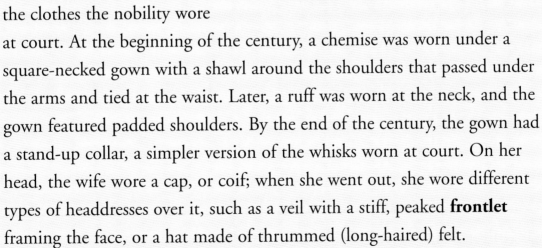

In the 17th century, flat white collars and high-crowned hats came into style, following the Puritans. These townswomen (left) wear lace-edged collars, while the Lord Mayor's wife (center) wears a stiff ruff.

place, which lasted from 1649 to 1659. However, in 1660, the monarchy was restored under Charles II.

The supporters of Cromwell, the Puritans, dressed in a plain, simple way. Their style of dress was in complete contrast to that of the Royalists, who wore flamboyant, brightly colored, rich clothing. The Puritans favored dark colors, such as black, brown, and gray. Instead of creating new fashions, they adapted existing styles. With their dark clothes, both men and women wore plain white linen collars and cuffs. The women also wore long white aprons over their gowns. On their heads, both sexes wore tall black hats made of felt. Women also wore white caps under their hats so that their hair was completely covered. In Wales, where the Puritan tradition was strong, the tall black hat and white cap came to be adopted as national dress for women.

## Frills, Flowers, and Ribbons

By the beginning of the 18th century, a middle class had been created that consisted of landed gentry, people below the nobility in rank, but still with substantial wealth. Since the time of Oliver Cromwell, the political power of this class had increased. To this group of people, such as gentleman farmers and city lawyers, was added a new group, wealthy traders, merchants, and businessmen involved in importing luxury goods, such as tea, coffee, and sugar, from the nation's colonies abroad. With the rising demand for these goods in the wealthy homes of Britain, fortunes were made, and the middle class became the most powerful political and economic force in the country.

Country squires (or gentlemen) wore long coats and vests, with knee breeches and stockings. Powdered wigs were worn either loose or tied at the back with a black bow and with a tricorne (three-cornered) hat on top. The squire's wife wore a gown that was a more-sophisticated version of an ordinary countrywoman's dress, with a flowered section at the front and a *fichu*, or small shawl, over the shoulders. She would also have worn a flat straw hat, decorated with flowers or ribbons, and decorative openwork mittens that left her fingers

**These gentlemen are wearing long coats and vests, along with knee-length breeches and stockings. The coats and vests are decorated in a style fitting for their social standing.**

uncovered. In the towns, these straw hats also became fashionable, along with many styles of bonnets. Indoors, both country- and townswomen wore a variety of ribboned and frilled mobcaps, especially for the popular social pastime of drinking tea and coffee.

## Gaiters and Top Hats

At the beginning of the 19th century, as transportation around the country became easier, both men and women began to wear practical travel clothes. Long, heavy woolen capes helped keep travelers warm, and tall hats protected their carefully arranged hairstyles. Men wore spatterdashes or gaiters, leather or

# Bloomers

Toward the end of the 19th century, women began to discard their long, heavy clothes for more practical wear, to the horror of many prudish commentators. Underneath their gowns, women wore pantalettes: long, lace-trimmed trousers that only children wore in public. In North America, Amelia Bloomer campaigned for women to wear a more substantial version of these for sporting activities. In Britain, these baggy trousers were adopted for cycling, which was considered very daring.

**The gentleman on the left is wearing a powdered wig, which has been adorned with a bow. The gentleman on the right is wearing a tricorne hat.**

cloth coverings buttoned over their trousers to protect them from muddy roads.

Hats were a great feature of the era. For men, the tall beaver hat with a buckle at the front gave way, in about 1818, to the familiar top hat. For women, hats ranged from the bibi bonnet, with its tall crown and large brim, to turbans with feathers and felt hats covered in bows. The hat became the most important single fashion item for women, and styles changed constantly.

During this period, the middle classes adopted similar styles of clothing to the nobility, because their income and social status now matched those of the upper class. Aristocrats and businessmen, both with their top hats and frock coats, were difficult to tell apart, and so were the ladies with their heavy, full-skirted gowns and elaborately decorated hats.

As factories began to produce garments on a mass scale, fashions began to change more quickly, creating a huge variety of clothing for consumers.

# Glossary

*Note: Specialized words relating to clothing are explained within the text, but those that appear more than once are listed below for easy reference.*

**Archaeologist** a person who studies history by analyzing the remains of past human cultures

**Bodice** the upper part of a woman's dress

**Bog** wet, spongy ground

**Breeches** short pants covering the hips and thighs and fitting snugly at the lower edges at or just below the knee

**Brooch** an ornament that is held by a pin or clasp and worn at or near the neck

**Chemise** a woman's one-piece undergarment

**Codpiece** a bag covering the male genitals and attached to his hose

**Corset** a woman's close-fitting undergarment that is often hooked and laced and that extends from beneath or above the bust or from the waist to below the hips

**Courtier** a person in attendance at the royal court

**Cravat** a band or scarf worn around the neck

**Doublet** a man's fitted jacket, with or without sleeves, sometimes padded and slashed with contrasting colors

**Farthingale** a support of hoops worn beneath a skirt to expand it at the hipline

**Feudal** an early European social system in which common people worked for a lord and were restricted to working on his land

**Frontlet** a band worn on the forehead

**Gore** a tapering or triangular piece of cloth

**Jet** a compact velvet-black coal that takes a good polish and is often used for jewelry

**Rosette** an ornament usually made of material gathered or pleated so that it resembles a rose

**Ruff** a large round collar of pleated muslin or linen

**Serf** a person in medieval times who was bound to the land and who served a lord as part of the feudal system

**Sinew** animal tendon used for cord or thread

**Slashing** slits in a garment designed to reveal a contrasting fabric underneath

**Toga** a loose outer garment

**Tunic** a simple slip-on garment made with or without sleeves and usually knee-length or longer, belted at the waist, and worn as an under or outer garment

# Timeline

| | |
|---|---|
| **9000 B.C.** | Early Stone Age. |
| **4000** | New Stone Age. |
| **2000** | Bronze Age. |
| **1000** | Iron Age. |
| **800** | Celts settle in Britain. |
| **A.D. 43–410** | Romans rule Britain. |
| **300** | Saxons settle in Britain, followed by Angles, Danes, Jutes, and Vikings. |
| **1066** | Normans conquer Britain. |
| **1154–1485** | Reign of the Plantaganet kings. |
| **1340–1400** | The poet Geoffrey Chaucer's lifespan. His most famous work, *The Canterbury Tales*, tells us a great deal about medieval dress. |
| **1485–1603** | Reign of the Tudor kings and queens. |
| **1603–1649** | Reign of the Stuart kings. |
| **1649–1659** | England becomes a republic (the Commonwealth). |
| **1660–1688** | Stuart kings are restored. |
| **1745** | The wearing of tartan and Highland dress is forbidden after the Jacobite uprising |
| **1714–1837** | Reign of the Hanoverian kings. |
| **1760** | The Industrial Revolution begins in Britain. |
| **1790** | The French Revolution topples the monarchy in France. |
| **1811** | The Englishman's top hat is adopted as universal style of dress for middle-class gentlemen. |
| **1837–1901** | Reign of Queen Victoria. |
| **1851** | Amelia Bloomer, an American, travels to London to publicize "bloomers." |
| **1856** | Crinoline introduced for women's clothing |
| **1870s** | The rear bustle becomes popular. |

# Online Sources

**Anglo-Saxon Living History 400-900 A.D.**
www.angelcynn.org.uk
Detailed information on all aspects of Anglo-Saxon culture. For information specifically on costume, follow the clothing link.

**History of the Kilt**
www.clan.com/history
History of Scottish dress.

**Ealaghol: The Isle of Skye Guide**
www.ealaghol.demon.co.uk
General information on the Celts, including Celtic history and mythology.

**Gallica: World of the Celts**
www.gallica.co.uk
Useful general site on Celtic culture, including a section on making your own Celtic clothing.

**Scotland Online**
www.tartans.scotland.net/
Information on all aspects of tartans, from making and weaving cloth to tracking down family names. Includes a register of all well-known tartans

# Further Reading

Boucher, François. *20,000 Years of Fashion: The History of Costume and Personal Adornment.* New York: Harry N. Abrams, 1987.

Fox, Lilla Margaret. *Costumes and Customs of the British Isles.* London: Chatto and Windus, 1974.

Gibson, Michael. *Everyday Life in Victorian Times.* Hemel Hempstead, England: Simon and Schuster, 1993.

Kennet, Frances. *World Dress: A Comprehensive Guide to the Folk Costume of the World.* London: Mitchell Beazley, 1994.

McDermott, Catherine. *Made in Britain: Tradition and Style in Contemporary British Fashion.* London: Mitchell Beazley, 2002.

Salariya, David. *Vikings and Their Travels.* Hemel Hempstead, England: Simon and Schuster, 1993.

Sichel, Marion. *History of Women's Costume.* London: Batsford Academic and Educational, 1984.

Yarwood, D J. *The Encyclopaedia of World Costume.* London: Batsford, 1978.

# About the Author

**Charlotte Greig** is a writer, broadcaster, and journalist. She has written on culture, literature, music, and history. She is the author of several books, and has written, researched, and presented programs for BBC Radio 4, and has contributed articles to national newspapers, *The Guardian* and *The Independent.* She has an MA in Intellectual History from Sussex

# Index